As Long As There Are Whales

As Long As There Are Whales

Evelyne Daigle

Illustrated by
Daniel Grenier

Translated by

Geneviève Wright

Tundra Books

Originally published in French as *Tant qu'il y aura des baleines . . .*
À la découverte des cétacés du Saint-Laurent by les éditions Les 400 Coups, Montreal, 2000
First published in this edition by Tundra Books, Toronto, 2004

Published in Canada by Tundra Books,
75 Sherbourne Street, Toronto, Ontario M5A 2P9

Published in the United States by Tundra Books of Northern New York,
P.O. Box 1030, Plattsburgh, New York 12901

Library of Congress Control Number: 2003113652

Library and Archives Canada Cataloguing in Publication

Daigle, Evelyne
        As long as there are whales / Evelyne Daigle ; illustrator, Daniel
Grenier; translator, Geneviève Wright.

Translation of: Tant qu'il y aura des baleines –
ISBN 0-88776-692-7

        1. Whales--Saint Lawrence River--Juvenile literature.
I. Grenier, Daniel II. Wright, Geneviève III. Title.

QL737.C4D3413 2004   j599.5'09713'7   C2003-905878-6

We acknowledge the financial support of the Government of Canada through the
Book Publishing Industry Development Program and that of the Government
of Ontario through the Ontario Media Development Corporation's Ontario Book
Initiative. We further acknowledge the support of the Canada Council for the
Arts and the Ontario Arts Council for our publishing program.

Design: Cindy Elisabeth Reichle

ISBN 13: 978-0-88776-692-3   ISBN 10: 0-88776-692-7

Printed and bound in China

2 3 4 5 6   10 09 08 07 06

To Marie-Jeanne
E.D.

To life, infinite source of wonder
D.G.

Notes on Measurements

To convert metric measurements to imperial terms, use the following tables.

Weight

1 metric ton = 1.1 short tons

1 kilogram = 2.2 pounds

1 gram = 0.04 ounce

Length

1 kilometer = 0.62 miles

1 meter = 39.37 inches

1 centimeter = 0.39 inches

1 millimeter = 0.04 inches

Contents

Discovering the Mysteries of the St. Lawrence

As soon as the ice leaves the St. Lawrence, the sea breeze begins to blow more gently. This is a sign of spring and the time when sailors feel called to the sea. Docks in the small villages along the coastline are teeming with life. Everyone is getting their boats ready, anxious to weigh anchor after a long hibernation.

Offshore, the first whales appear, another sure sign of the change of season. They are humpback whales, weary after a long journey from the Caribbean. A mother and her calf have finally reached their destination and main feeding area after a three or four thousand kilometer trip.

The calf is discovering the St. Lawrence River for the first time, so it sticks close to its mother. This is the first migration of its life. All these new sensations! Why did they have to leave the clear, turquoise, tropical waters where it was born the winter before? Why launch off on this long expedition, where eddies and currents get colder and colder the

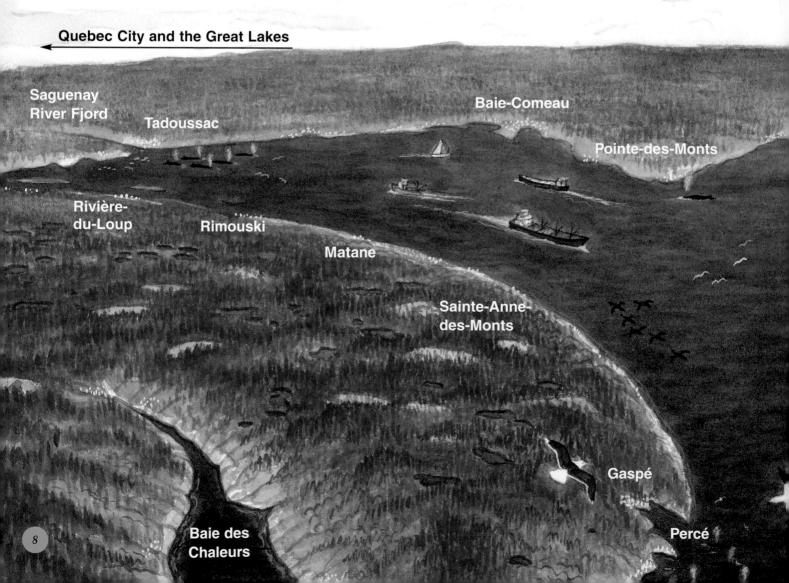

← Quebec City and the Great Lakes

Saguenay River Fjord

Tadoussac

Baie-Comeau

Pointe-des-Monts

Rivière-du-Loup

Rimouski

Matane

Sainte-Anne-des-Monts

Gaspé

Baie des Chaleurs

Percé

farther north they go? In the freezing waters of the St. Lawrence, the young whale needs to be in constant communication with its mother. The water is so opaque, the seaweed and plankton so dense, that it cannot afford to lose sight of her. It wonders where on earth its mother has brought it? The salty taste of the sea is the only thing it recognizes from home.

Odd-looking birds – seagulls, northern gannets, and cormorants – dive-bomb it every time it comes up for a breath, making it feel even more insecure.

The calf finds the currents in the St. Lawrence surprisingly powerful, just like the currents along the coast of North America. The tides weren't even that strong out at sea. And the sounds intrigue it. They're all so different, and from every direction. They come from boats sailing in the river; there are more boats here than on the ocean. Suddenly, through the currents, it spots a school of capelin. It has never seen so many fish in its life! The mother heads straight for the cloud of small fish and swallows a huge quantity of them. The young whale will have to do the same one day, when it is no longer getting its mother's milk.

Everything is so new for this young humpback. It is suddenly beginning to see why its mother insisted on this great migration. They stopped along the way a few times to feed, but now the calf understands that the icy, turbulent waters of the majestic St. Lawrence are actually one of the most extraordinary pantries on the planet.

Sept-Îles

Havre-Saint-Pierre

Anticosti Island

Atlantic Ocean

Below the Surface

The St. Lawrence River starts in the freshwater of the Great Lakes. Gradually, it becomes a river, an estuary, and finally, a gulf. From the Great Lakes to the Quebec City area, the St. Lawrence is a freshwater river. Then sea water slowly begins to filter in, the water becomes brackish, and the river becomes an estuary. The water from the Atlantic Ocean enters with such force that it carries salt water as far up as the mouth of the Saguenay River, and the St. Lawrence River becomes the St. Lawrence Estuary. At Pointe-des-Monts, on the north shore, and Sainte-Anne-des-Monts, on the south shore, the St. Lawrence widens and becomes a gulf.

Mysterious landscapes lie below the surface of the water. Endless underwater valleys, mountains, and plains are unknown to land dwellers. Although the depths are dark, whales are very familiar with this underwater landscape and navigate in and around it very smoothly.

These formations become corridors – obstacles for the water of the St. Lawrence, which is in constant motion. Currents, undercurrents, and tides are

Quebec City and the Great Lakes ←

0 m

Tadoussac

100 m

Cloud of zooplankton

Why does water go up and down?

All this marine life is rocked continuously by the never-ending rhythm of the tides. Every day there are two high tides and two low tides in the Estuary and the Gulf. Tides are the result of the gravitational pull of the moon as it revolves around the Earth. Tides are higher in the Estuary, where the St. Lawrence is narrower. They can be as high as six meters and are slightly lower in the Gulf.

200 m

300 m

continuously stirring up the river. Sailors and navigators can tell you all about it!

There is an enormous underwater cliff in the St. Lawrence Estuary. Sea water pours in from the Atlantic, hits the cliff, and rises to the surface. On the way, it scoops up nutrients from the bottom of the sea. These nutrients are critical for fertilizing microscopic algae on the surface of the water. They are the first link in the ocean food chain.

The algae then feed all the other links in the food chain. Wherever water from the bottom of the ocean rises to the surface, you will find food-rich areas where sea animals abound. The world over, fish, birds, seals, and whales gather in these places every summer to feed. So the movement of the water in the St. Lawrence creates enough sea life to satisfy everyone's hunger.

Atlantic Ocean →

Pointe-des-Monts

School of fish

Where does the salt in the sea come from?

The salt in the sea does not come from a secret mine, buried deep in the ocean floor. It actually comes from the earth! Rainwater picks up fine dust from rock as it falls, which is then carried to the nearest body of water. The stream then follows its normal course to the sea. All these waterways carrying tiny particles of rock give the sea its salty taste. The seawater that evaporates in the sun is replaced by rainwater, which means that the level of salinity in the ocean has been stable for about 200 million years.

A Feast for Whales

The salty waters of the St. Lawrence are teeming with richly diverse sea life. Whales, starfish, salmon, and seabirds are all part of different food chains in which nothing happens by accident.

All this life starts in the springtime. As the first rays of sunlight hit the St. Lawrence, phytoplankton – microscopic plants that live suspended in the water – begin to multiply. Billions and billions of them suddenly come to life. Microscopic animals called zooplankton, which also live in the water, feed on all these tiny plants. There are billions of tons of them in the water. However, the lifespan of zooplankton is fairly short – schools of capelin and smelt soon gobble them up.

Spring is also when whales arrive in the St. Lawrence. They are eager to take part in the feast.

Whales are at the top of the food chain and have enormous food requirements. A fin whale, for example, can eat up to two tons of food a day!

Toothed whales and baleen whales have developed very different adaptations to meet their need for food. Some whales capture their prey with their teeth. They are called Odontocetes or toothed whales. They have only one nostril, called a blowhole, on the top of their head. Rorqual whales have baleen plates instead of teeth and they are known as Mysticetes or baleen whales. They have a double blowhole. The fin whale is a Mysticete often found in the St. Lawrence. Killer whales are Odontocetes and, although they do visit occasionally, they are a more rare sight in the Gulf of St. Lawrence.

---

fin whale
Balaenoptera physalus

Length : 20 meters
Weight : 70 tons

The right side of the jaw is white, the left side is dark gray.

Odontocete Strategy

Odontocetes use their sharp powerful teeth for grabbing fairly decent-sized prey (ten centimeters or more) that happen to cross their path. Fish and mollusks (little animals that live inside shells) are on their menu. The teeth of Odontocetes are designed for grabbing prey one at a time, but not for chewing.

Killer whales are formidable hunters that attack their prey in packs, like wolves. These carnivores have a wide-ranging diet: fish, birds, seals, and even other cetaceans! They are whales' only predators and play an important role in the food chain. They help to keep a balance among the species.

In the ocean, small animals always keep an eye out for bigger ones. Herring love munching on young capelin but must be on constant alert for cod, who keep a lookout for seals on the prowl for their next meal. And seals have their own predators to deal with.

orca or killer whale
Orcinus orca

Length : 7 meters
Weight : 6 tons

Zooplankton

Phytoplankton

Mysticete Strategy

The minke whale is the smallest of the Mysticetes. The word *Mysticete* comes from Greek and Latin meaning *mustached whale*. The mustache refers to the baleen plates, which are found where teeth would be. A fringelike sieve of baleen hangs down from the palate of the minke whale and filters the enormous amount of food the whale takes in.

Like all rorqual whales, the minke whale has a very effective technique for taking in great quantities of zooplankton, small fish, and salt water. Ventral grooves on the underside of its throat and chest help to expand its gigantic mouth (which is probably as big as the room you're in now). It then expels all the salt water, forcing it out through the baleen plates with its powerful tongue. Zooplankton and fish become trapped in the very tight sieve formed by the baleen plates, only to be swept up by the hungry minke's agile tongue.

Try to picture this: if a krill weighs less than two grams and a rorqual needs two tons of krill every day, that means that the whale is taking in over one million tiny shrimp in seventy-three filtrations!

There is one exception: the blue whale feeds exclusively on krill, tiny little shrimplike animals that are concentrated in huge, thick clouds, sometimes stretching for several kilometers.

minke whale
Balaenoptera acutorostrata

Length : 8 meters
Weight : 7 tons
White band on top side of pectoral fin

Baleen are a series of horny plates, about twenty-five to sixty centimeters in length, triangular in shape, made of the same material that forms our own fingernails. Rigid hairs extend from each plate and act as a sieve to trap food.

Mysticetes have between 200 and 450 baleen plates suspended from each side of the mouth, spaced about five to ten millimeters apart so that their tiny prey cannot escape. The shortest baleen plates are at the front of the whale's mouth and the longest at the back.

Right whales have baleen that are two to three meters long, but their technique for capturing zooplankton is very different because they don't have any ventral grooves.

Baleen plate

Baleen plates

The Ancestor

The ancestor of whales and dolphins lived 55 million years ago, shortly after the dinosaurs disappeared. The Mesonyx was a carnivorous land mammal about the size of a dog, with small hooves instead of claws. It lived in tropical climates, along the edges of lagoons and estuaries. How did it end up in the sea? It must have been drawn to the rich food in the water when competition with other land mammals became too stiff. The water offered food resources that mammals had not yet discovered. Over the course of the next few million years, the body of the Mesonyx gradually transformed and became perfectly adapted to life in the water, but without becoming a fish!

It wasn't until 25 million years ago that whales and dolphins appeared in their current form. Whales and dolphins belong to the order Cetacea.

Compare the body of a white-sided dolphin, which visits the St. Lawrence every summer, to that of the Mesonyx.

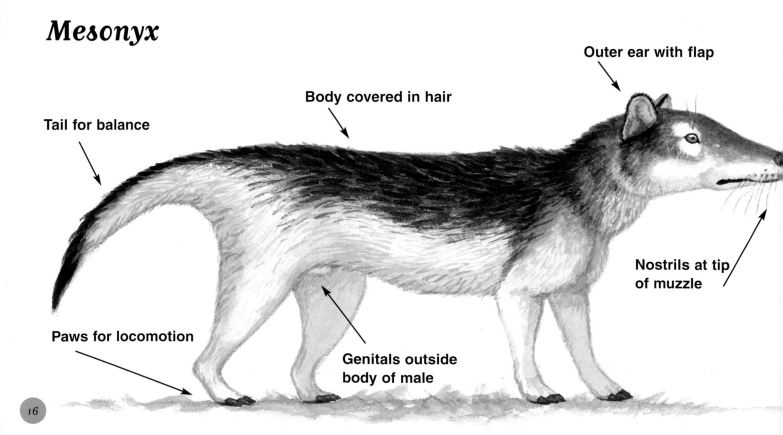

Tail (or caudal fin) for propulsion

Mesonyx

Outer ear with flap

Body covered in hair

Tail for balance

Nostrils at tip of muzzle

Paws for locomotion

Genitals outside body of male

16

White-Sided Dolphin

No hair on skin for
better hydrodynamics

Genitals inside body
to cut down resistance,
even in male.

Front paws transformed into
pectoral fins for balance

Nostrils (called
blowholes) migrated
to top of head for
easier breathing

External ear only
a small hole

According to researchers, whales sleep floating
on the water's surface with their blowholes
out of the water for breathing. They keep
their balance by fluttering their fins slightly,
and their thick layer of blubber helps them
to float effortlessly. Scientists have observed
that some whales sleep for thirty minutes at
a time, six or seven times a day, while others
nap for two hours at a time. The length of
sleep depends on whether they are migrating
or resting. Unfortunately, boats sometimes
collide with whales while they are sleeping
because they are barely visible on the surface
of the water.

Atlantic white-sided dolphin
Lagenorhynchus acutus

Length : 2 meters
Weight : 150 kilograms

Yellow patch at rear of body

Built for the Water

Why Are Whales So Big?

At four tons, the elephant is the biggest land animal we know of today. At seventy-five tons, the Brachiosaurus was one of the largest dinosaurs. But of all the animals that have ever lived on earth, none has rivaled the blue whale in either size or weight. The environment in which it lives has allowed it to reach gigantic proportions: the blue whale weighs approximately 100 tons!

Water supports weight much more easily than air. As a result, whales have expanded in size because they are not limited by gravity. They have a layer of blubber ten to twenty centimeters thick that makes them buoyant and allows them to live in weightlessness like astronauts.

Whale or Boat?

What do a boat and a whale have in common? The first boatbuilders must have been inspired by the shape of cetaceans. Whales are streamlined at both ends, which lets them glide through the water easily, with no resistance.

The pectoral fins (or flippers) on either side of the body help to stabilize them, like the keel of a boat, and the horizontal tailfin (or flukes) propels them forward. Cetaceans are hydrodynamic, just like boats, which allows them to cut through waves.

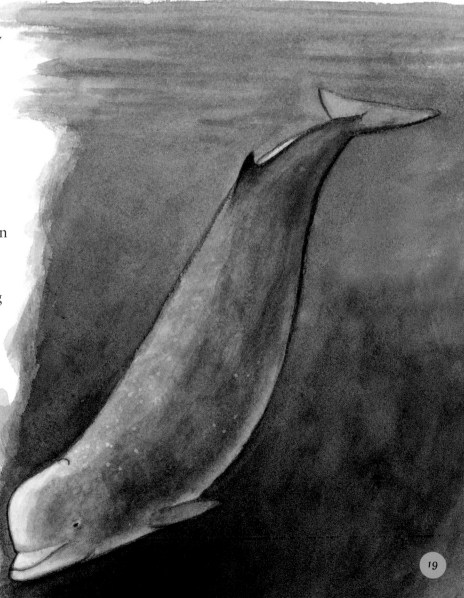

northern bottlenose whale
Hyperoodon ampullatus

Length : 8 meters
Weight : 3 tons

Diving to the Depths

Northern bottlenose whales are wonderful divers, as are sperm whales. They can stay submerged for up to seventy minutes at a time and can dive as deep as 800 meters! Cetaceans are mammals, so they have lungs. Proportionally, their lungs are smaller than those of humans. So, how do they manage to beat all the diving records?

When a northern bottlenose whale comes to the surface to breathe, it exhales and then inhales ninety percent of all the air its lungs can contain, as opposed to seventy-five percent for humans. It has more available oxygen than we do because it is better at emptying and refilling its lungs, not because its lungs contain more air.

The oxygen captured during inhalation is then stored in its blood in a protein called hemoglobin. Cetaceans have a higher volume of blood than humans, so they have more hemoglobin in their blood vessels and muscles. This means they can accumulate more oxygen reserves and stay under water longer!

Seeing with Their Ears

Animals, like humans, explore the world with their senses. A dog uses its sense of smell to find out who has been on its territory; a penguin recognizes its partner's cry out of all the others; and a great horned owl can spot a mouse in the dark from a great distance using night vision. Human beings use their vision more than any other sense to move around in their environment and to meet their needs. Hearing is the best guide for whales in their dark, odorless universe filled with a multitude of different sounds.

Sound travels much better in water than in air. That is why, as they evolved, cetaceans developed their hearing and an echolocation system to communicate, navigate, and locate their prey in the darkness of their underwater world.

Cetaceans communicate using a series of sounds, some of which are inaudible to the human ear. The white-beaked dolphin, which summers in the Gulf of St. Lawrence, makes a variety of different sounds ranging from squeals and clicks to moans and groans, depending on the purpose. The sounds it makes when it is on the hunt, on the move, and at rest are all different.

white-beaked dolphin
Lagenorhynchus albirostris

Length : 2.5 meters
Weight : 200 kilograms

We know very little about the connection between the sounds whales make and their behavior. However, we do know that cetaceans generally vocalize more when they are engaged in intense social contact. Their highly developed language strengthens the bonds within their pods.

The whale's song is a series of organized sounds, repeated over and over. The humpback whale is one of the rare species that sings during its mating display. Generally, males vocalize to intimidate other males and to drive them out of their territory. Female right whales are an exception because they also sing. Other species of whale let out cries, grunts, or sounds that are not organized enough to be considered songs.

In captivity, experiments with dolphin and beluga sounds have shown that these animals can tell the difference between small objects from a great distance and even between objects that are similar, but not identical. Whales and dolphins are often thought to be particularly intelligent because of the size of their brain. What we do know is that their brain has developed the hearing and touch functions particularly well.

Echo from the Deep

Echolocation is a method of transmitting and receiving very complex sounds. It is a way of sending and receiving messages. Echolocation works the same way sonar does on a submarine. Whales and dolphins use it to detect obstacles and to find prey in turbid water or at depths where no light penetrates. They send out a sound in a specific direction, the sound waves hit an object or obstacle and are reflected back, giving the animals a mental picture of a school of fish or a rock in their path.

The resulting image is so precise that it even gives them a reading of the texture, shape, and thickness of things around them. Beluga whales have the most accurate sonar.

Sounds emitted by cetaceans travel great distances. This means that they can communicate over hundreds of kilometers. Blue whales hold the record for emitting the lowest frequency sounds, which travel the farthest. Their sounds can travel up to a thousand kilometers!

Using echolocation, a dolphin can detect a school of fish at 100 meters.

There is a theory that the sperm whale, a massive animal with a large squarish head, produces ultrasounds powerful enough to stun prey. Although giant squid are faster swimmers, sperm whales have been known to feed on them. Their remains have been found in the stomachs of sperm whales.

sperm whale
Physeter macrocephalus

Length : 15 meters
Weight : 30 tons
Average dive time: 30 minutes

Cetaceans do not have vocal chords. Instead, they make sounds by displacing air contained in sacs behind their forehead.

The reflected sounds, or echoes, are received in the fat-filled lower jawbone. The sound travels to the inner ear and then to the brain, where the information is decoded.

Cetaceans have extremely sensitive hearing and water carries sound very well. Their acoustic environment is filled with a multitude of different noises. Be it wind, rain, ice, cargo ships, pleasure crafts, or sonar, cetaceans take it all in and are fully aware of human activity on the St. Lawrence.

Does human recreation disturb whales? Does noise from boats interfere with their echolocation system, hindering their search for food? Do the frequencies emitted by motors scramble their communication? Are whales becoming deaf? We have no definite proof that human activity disturbs whales but we have good reason to think that our activities affect theirs, so we must be cautious.

giant squid
Architeuthis dux

Length : Between 12 and 17 meters (including tentacles)

It squirts black ink on its enemy as a means of defense.

Sound waves emitted by the sperm whale

Echo sent back by the squid

Big Love

When mating season arrives, a whale's energy is focused entirely on looking for partners to reproduce with, to ensure continuation of the species.

Reproduction happens in warm or temperate waters. A male's courting strategy includes songs, vocalizations, and sounds designed to make its presence felt by other males. Despite all the studies, little is actually known about the meaning of their songs.

Touch is another aspect of the mating display. Cetaceans have a highly developed sense of touch. There is a lot of physical contact, caressing, and nibbling between male and female individuals, particularly among dolphins.

There is a great deal of competition among males before mating can occur. In certain species, individuals do serious combat and only the strongest prevail. With right whales, there is a free-for-all as males compete for the same female.

When the female consents, the closest male sticks his belly up against her to mate. Then another does the same, and another, and another, until the most persistent male succeeds in passing on his genes to the next generation. Mating is brief but very frequent.

The mating season for right whales is crucial because the survival of this endangered species depends on it. The Bay of Fundy in New Brunswick is a breeding and calving ground for the 325 individuals that make up the only remaining right whale population in the North Atlantic. It is critical that we ensure the survival of this very fragile whale herd. Right whales are rare visitors to the St. Lawrence.

Male and female cetaceans have very few external features to help us tell them apart. With the large rorquals, females are slightly bigger than males, but it is the opposite with toothed whales. Killer whales are the exception – their long dorsal fin looks different on the female.

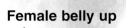
Female belly up

right whale
Eubalaena glacialis

Length : 15 meters
Weight : 50 tons

Callosities on head
Status: Endangered

25

Coming into The World Tail First

Cetaceans are mammals, so whale embryos develop inside the female's body. After a gestation period ranging from ten to fifteen months, depending on the species, a female whale gives birth to a calf, which comes out tail first. As soon as calves are born, their mothers urge them to the surface to grab their first breath of air through the blowholes on the top of their head.

Suckling . . . Under Water?

A mother steers her newborn under her belly to feed from the mammary glands found on either side of the genital slit. The mother squirts rich, warm milk into the baby's mouth. The calf will feed on mother's milk for seven to twelve months, at which time it will begin to eat its first solid food. By imitating its mother, the calf learns the best way and the best places to find food and will gradually become independent.

Between birth and the time it first migrates to northern waters, a calf has to become very strong. Its growth rate is phenomenal. At six months, the calf will have reached half its adult size, which a human does not reach until the age of two.

After the migration to feeding areas, a mother will temporarily abandon her calf to feed and build up her reserves of fat again. She will have eaten virtually nothing since the calf was born. All her energy will have been focused on nurturing the baby, which is an exhausting job. So she arrives at the summer feeding area very depleted. In the fall, she will be ready once again to take the journey in the opposite direction and return to the breeding ground, where the cycle of life begins again.

Unfortunately, the birth rate among cetaceans is low. A female only reproduces every two or three years, which means that rebuilding herd populations is slow. One example is the right whale, which has suffered from overhunting in years past.

Cetacean's milk is very rich in protein and fat. The fat content in some whales' milk is as high as forty percent. By comparison, cow's milk contains three to four percent fat.

Bubbles and Fun

Humans have always tried to understand the behavior of animals around them. Marine mammals, like whales, don't make it easy. Cetaceans live primarily under the water, and only a small part of their life can be seen from the surface of the sea. A circle of bubbles on the water or a fluke slap are sometimes the only clues researchers have to tell them what is happening under the sea.

The hunting behavior of humpback whales is quite remarkable. They use a technique called bubble netting to herd and capture their prey. Humpbacks puff air from their blowholes under the water while swimming in a spiral formation. This creates a screen of bubbles that encloses the school of fish they're after. The fish become frightened and move closer together, trapped in a net of bubbles.

The humpbacks then dive down and come up with their mouth wide open, snatching the column of trapped fish on the way. Birds will often try to get in on the free meal too!

Some species of whale, such as humpbacks, are very active. Sometimes they will stick just their heads out of the water (called spy hopping) as though they were on the lookout for something, or hit the surface of the water with a pectoral fin or their fluke. Sometimes, they will even propel themselves completely out of the water. This is called breaching. Are they just playing? Giving a warning? Trying to be intimidating? Or just getting rid of the parasites that live on their body? One thing we do know for sure is that all activity of this kind is part of the way whales communicate.

Animals have to constantly meet their vital needs – to look for food, to protect themselves and their young, to find a partner to reproduce with. Whales meet some of their basic survival needs through their behaviors on the water's surface. However, science still has many unanswered questions about their behavior.

humpback whale
Megaptera novaeangliae

Length : 15 meters
Weight : 30 tons

The whale gets its name from the hump underneath the dorsal fin.
Status: Endangered

Stranding

Humans have always been puzzled by whales that run aground and die on shore. Why do whales do this?

Cetaceans found on the shore of the St. Lawrence are often animals that died at sea and washed up on the beach. Usually they have died of old age or illness or had an accident with a boat. Sometimes pilot whales, which are small and black in color, strand alive by the hundreds on the shores of Newfoundland.

Researchers are trying to find a scientific explanation for this behavior. Theories vary from case to case. They have observed, for example, that when they try to put old or sick whales back in the water, these individuals come back and run aground. The theory is that whales probably strand in groups because they are following a leader. The first beached individual sends out distress signals that alert the rest of the group who, unfortunately, respond by joining their companion.

Other explanations have been offered. It may be that whales have parasites or infections in their ears that disrupt their echolocation system. Without echolocation, which helps them to know their environment and to navigate in it, they may be knocked off course end up on shore.

Whales can also become beached after a storm. Imagine a whale hunting a school of fish in shallow water near a gently sloping shoreline. Water churned up by the storm might make it hard for the whale to use its sonar system. It might then fail to recognize the edge of the water and run aground.

In any event, the number of strandings each year is negligible compared to the number of whales in the oceans of the world. So this is not an alarming phenomenon. Based on current scientific understanding, the mass suicide theory has been pretty well ruled out.

pilot whale
Globicephala melas

Length : 6 meters
Weight : 2 tons

From the Biggest to the Smallest

The St. Lawrence is home to the largest and the smallest cetaceans in the world: the blue whale and the harbor porpoise. The blue whale is the biggest animal on the planet, larger than any dinosaur that ever roamed the Earth.

To give you an idea of its size, if you were to close the book you are holding, the width of the book would be equal to the diameter of the blue whale's eye – and it has small eyes for its size!

Did you know that, despite its size, the blue whale has a predator? The killer whale! A small group of killer whales can surround and attack a great blue whale.

A porpoise's size has advantages and disadvantages. A harbor porpoise can catch fast swimmers like herring and mackerel because it moves so quickly through the water. However, because it is so small, it often gets caught in fishnets while going after the same prey as fishermen.

In contrast, the great blue whale is so huge that it has trouble simply rolling over. If it can find a school of krill, which can be several kilometers long, that makes its life much easier!

harbour porpoise
Phocoena phocoena

Length : 1.5 meters
Weight : 40 to 50 kilograms

Statistics on Blue Whales in the St. Lawrence

• Their average weight is estimated at approximately 100 tons, the equivalent of twenty-five elephants.
• Their average length is approximately thirty meters.
• Newborns are about seven meters long and weigh 2500 kilograms.
• A baby blue whale drinks 225 liters of milk per day, with a fat content of forty percent.
• A calf grows at an incredible rate of about ninety kilograms a day, or three to four kilograms an hour when it is feeding on its mother's milk – a newborn almost grows before your very eyes.
• An adult eats up to four tons of krill a day in the summer.
• A blue whale can live for forty to fifty years.

blue whale
Balaenoptera musculus

Length : 30 meters
Weight : 100 tons

Blue-gray color
Status: Endangered

The St. Lawrence Beluga

Encountering a beluga whale is a real privilege. A somewhat ghostly animal, the beluga is a symbol of fragility and vulnerability. It knows the St. Lawrence like no other because it lives there year-round. The beluga herd in the St. Lawrence River is the only one in the world that does not live in the Arctic. The St. Lawrence provides habitat similar to the Arctic: the salt water is nice and cold and there is lots of food.

There are many beluga herds in the Canadian North. The total beluga population is over 100,000. Other Arctic beluga herds live in northern Russia, Norway, Greenland, and Alaska.

A beluga has all the characteristics of a polar animal. Its white color acts as camouflage in the ice. It has a bumpy ridge extending along its back, instead of a dorsal fin, that allows it to break through the ice to breathe without injuring itself. Belugas have a flexible neck, while all other whales have fused cervical vertebrae and cannot turn their head.

Belugas are highly social animals, which explains their extensive vocabulary. They have developed some of the most varied vocal repertoires in the animal kingdom. From its rounded forehead, a beluga sends out ultrasound waves to find its food.

The beluga herd in the St. Lawrence is not what it was a hundred years ago. At the turn of the last century, there were over 5,000 belugas in the River. Their numbers have dropped considerably since then. They were overhunted because it was thought that they were eating the salmon and cod that humans needed to survive. Authorities even offered a bonus of fifteen dollars for every beluga tail brought in, to encourage elimination of the species as quickly as possible. The hunt was not brought to an end until the nineteen seventies. Now, there are between 700 and 1,200 in the St. Lawrence herd and the beluga is an endangered species.

Nowadays, because scientists have raised the alarm, the St. Lawrence beluga is protected. However, damage to its habitat and pollution continue to threaten its well-being.

The beluga is affected by various illnesses, but the link between disease and pollutants has yet to be found. Contaminants are not biodegradable, so the only way that belugas can get rid of them is through the female. A mother can reduce the level of pollutants in her body through her milk, but a newborn beluga starts life contaminated.

For all these reasons, the health of the St. Lawrence beluga is a concern. It will take generations, many more studies, and a lot of determination to improve the situation. The beluga's health is definitely a reflection of the state of the St. Lawrence River.

beluga whale
Delphinapterus leucas

Length : 4 meters
Weight : 1.5 tons

Calf (newborn): dark brown
Bluecalf (yearling): blue-gray
Gray (two-year-old): light gray
Life span: 25 to 30 years

The Oil Rush

For centuries, whales in the St. Lawrence River and the oceans of the world were viewed as man's only means of subsistence. Hunters would risk their lives in their small whaleboats to confront the creature so key to their survival. Whalers were both fascinated and frightened by their massive yet mysterious prey.

Whalers had to know the habits of whales intimately, to find and identify them, and to figure out their migration routes. Basically, whale hunters were interested in the large whales: rorqual whales, right whales, and especially sperm whales.

Wherever whales could be found close to shore, whalers were never far behind. Europeans were the first to make whaling an occupation. They traveled in large sailing ships equipped with wooden canoes. As soon as a whale was spotted, the canoe was lowered into the water, and rowers, helmsmen, and harpooners would jump onboard. They would head straight for their prey, hoping to emerge victorious – and still alive – after the confrontation between man and beast.

In modern times, basic whaling techniques were replaced by more advanced methods, which gave whalers a definite advantage over their prey. The harpoons were launched from cannons and would explode under the whale's skin. The whale blubber would be transformed into oil on a factory ship. The fat would be rendered in specially designed ovens and stored in barrels.

The greatest destruction of whale herds occurred between the end of the nineteenth century and the nineteen thirties. Tens of thousands of whales were slaughtered throughout the oceans of the world. It was the oil rush.

In northern Canada, the Inuit still have the privilege of hunting whale because they need this resource to survive and to feed their families. The meat and blubber give them important proteins and vitamins.

"Porpoise" Hunting

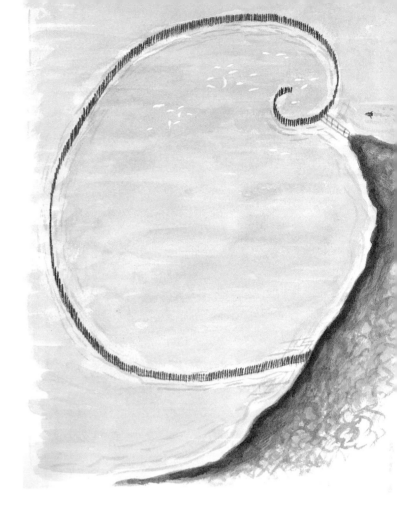

The St. Lawrence beluga was not protected from hunting until 1979. Whalers had an ingenious way of using the tides to capture the small whales they used to call "white porpoises." They would plant thousands of stakes in a semicircle, stretching from the shore out to sea. At high tide, belugas chasing fish near shore would swim into the trap. Although there were no nets or gates to keep them there, they couldn't escape. They were prisoners. The hunters would wait until low tide to harpoon the belugas and tow them back to shore. Because belugas are very social and usually move in groups, whalers could take over a hundred belugas in one tide.

Products of the Hunt

Whale oil became another gold mine, but the meat and baleen were also highly valued. The oil was used to light street lamps or lanterns in lighthouses, and the baleen (or whalebone) was used to make umbrella ribs and to stiffen the corsets of well-dressed women. The hide from some species, like beluga, was used to make very tough leather.

Today the whale rush is practically over. Whale products have been replaced by less expensive synthetics, but hunting has declined primarily because attitudes have changed. Now we understand that every species is essential to the balance of our ecosystems.

To solve the problem of dramatically declining populations, whale hunting was banned by the International Whaling Commission in 1986. However, there are still some exceptions. Countries like Japan, Norway, and Russia have continued to practice controlled whaling, and Iceland joined them recently. We must remain on guard because the lure of profit is a constant threat to whales' survival.

Studying Cetaceans

The study of whales is a fascinating occupation. In fact, it's more than an occupation, it's a way of life. There are many professions involved in the study of cetaceans. Biologists do their work at sea, but others, like geneticists, physicists, mathematicians, and chemists, work behind the scenes. They complement biologists' work and provide precious information on the health of whales and their herds.

The St. Lawrence River is a very demanding work environment for biologists and anyone else who sails it. People who study whales often do so in small boats, so they have to be very careful. Like sailors, they must constantly be on the lookout for changes in the weather. When the wind picks up (signaling an approaching storm), the waves swell, or fog moves in, they know that they must leave the observation area and head back to shore. Patience is a key ingredient in studying whales. You have to wait for them to surface to

breathe in order to catch little snippets of their lives. Despite these limitations, researchers have developed various ways of exploring the mysterious world of whales – a little at a time.

Their working tools consist of a camera, binoculars, a hydrophone, a crossbow with specially designed arrows, a notebook, and … a boat! Biologists have to be sharpshooters, photographers, and captains all in one!

Scientists hope to learn many things from their research. They want to know how many whales, and which species of whale, summer in the St. Lawrence. They want to understand their movements and diving habits. They want to determine their sex and how they are related to one another. They want to make connections between the sounds they make and their behavior on the surface … and more.

Photo-Identification

Recognizing each animal individually is a critical part of any study of animal behavior. To be counted, animals must be identified one by one. A process called photo-identification is used to do this with whales. It involves photographing distinctive features on each animal. Scars, nicks, or natural markings on their skin provide very good clues for identifying whales without disturbing them. In the past twenty years, scientists have identified more than 350 different blue whales in the St. Lawrence.

Marine biologists use the photos they have taken at sea to put together a catalog of whale pictures. They give each animal a name and a code number.

Getting to Know Each Whale

How does one know for certain whether a whale is a male or a female? Who are its parents, brothers, sisters, and cousins? Observing its behavior on the surface does not give enough information. To reveal a whale's history, biologists take a sample, or superficial biopsy, of the animal's skin, which does not harm the whale in any way. Using a crossbow and a special arrow with a hollow dart, they take a small piece of skin and blubber from the animal's side. Then they send the sample to the laboratory, which provides information about the whale. Genetics reveals the whale's sex and what

Whenever a new whale appears in the St. Lawrence, its photo is compared to the others in the catalog. This lets researchers keep track of the changes (or population dynamics) in whale herds that visit the Estuary and the Gulf of St. Lawrence, and even to follow their migratory routes back to their winter homes.

family it comes from. A little sample of blubber shows how many pollutants the whale has built up in its body throughout its lifetime. Of course, they have to take a picture of the whale before they do a biopsy because they wouldn't want to sample the same animal twice.

The underside of a humpback's tail is like a fingerprint. No two humpback tails are alike. Photo-identification is also used to identify giraffes and zebras by their spots and stripes.

Satellite Tracking

Scientists have many important questions about the way these marine mammals live. How deep can a whale dive? How long can it stay under? How fast does it swim? What are its movements in a given season? It is difficult to follow the same whale for a whole summer or to dive with it, so scientists have found another way of answering their questions. They attach a radio transmitter to the whale's back with a suction cup. The sound waves created by the device are sent up to a satellite, which bounces them back to a receiver, which is hooked up to computers that are able to interpret the information. Over time, the device just falls off on its own without harming the whale.

Listening to Whales

Some researchers specialize in bio-acoustics, or the relationship between the sounds whales make and their behavior. A hydrophone makes it possible to listen to their sounds. A hydrophone is a very sensitive microphone that is resistant to salt water. Other scientists use microphones placed on the floor of the Atlantic Ocean to identify whale sounds among all the other sounds in the sea and to track whales during their seasonal migrations.

Studying cetaceans is a fascinating occupation. To understand whales' movements, it takes hours and hours of observation at sea, year in and year out. If you have sea legs, every encounter with a whale or a pod of dolphins is a joy and an adventure. Wind, fog, cold, and salty water are all part of the excitement of studying whales. There are two things you must have to become a good cetologist: scientific rigor and a passion for the sea.

The Story of Pseudo

Since 1982, biologists at the Mingan Island Cetacean Study research station have been tracking a female humpback whale they have named Pseudo. Pseudo had a calf called Fleuret, identified as a female, who has had two calves herself. After Fleuret, Pseudo had another little female called Alpha; unfortunately, she was found dead in a fishnet off the coast near Sept-Îles. After Alpha, Pseudo had a third and then a fourth calf, whose gender has not yet been determined. Pseudo is a regular in the Gulf of St. Lawrence, just like Ebène, Nocturne, Splish, Spine, and Brax.

For Whales to Survive

The St. Lawrence flows from the Great Lakes to the Atlantic Ocean. It is one of the most important rivers in the world. It provides drinking water for most of the province of Quebec and is used for sport fishing and other recreational activities. Boats from around the world use the seaway. Industries, farms, towns, and villages dot its shores. Human presence around the St. Lawrence has significantly altered the surrounding landscape and has generated the pollution that is harming whales today.

Every minute of every day, pollutants are pouring into the St. Lawrence. They are odorless and colorless. When pollutants enter the water, they settle on the river bottom, where they are gobbled up by fish, squid, shrimp, and other animals that the belugas eat. Because they are at the top of the food chain, belugas build up huge concentrations of pollutants that can lead to a whole variety of illnesses. The health of the belugas is a good indicator of the quality of the water in the St. Lawrence River.

Fortunately, efforts have been made in recent years to reduce the amount of pollution being dumped in the St. Lawrence. However, it takes time for the traces of pollution in an animal's body to disappear. What can you do to help? Take a look around at the things that cause pollution in your own life (at home, at school, at work). Where does your garbage go? What happens to dangerous household products (spent batteries, leftover paint, used oil)? Do you try to avoid consuming too

Plastic bags were found in the stomach of a beached whale that died after swallowing them.

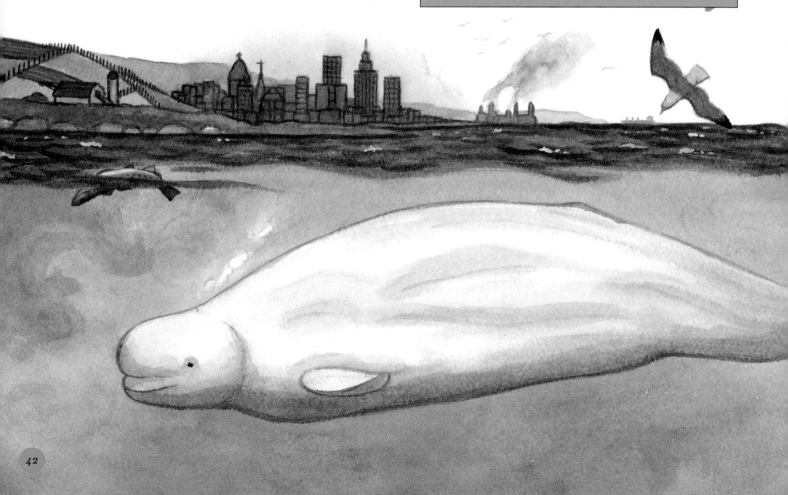

much? Although the little things we can do every day to protect the environment may not seem like much, they really do help to clean up the water in the St. Lawrence River.

Heading out in a boat on the St. Lawrence to watch whales is often an unforgettable experience. Hearing a whale breathe, witnessing its incredible power and agility in the water, or catching a whiff of its breath – which can be revolting – are all things that stay in one's memory for a long time.

When we admire the beauty of these animals, we can easily forget our responsibility toward them. We do not yet fully understand how human activity affects whales. It is difficult to determine whether vessels on the St. Lawrence disturb whales or not. One thing we do know is that the amount of boat traffic has increased considerably in the past ten years, and we must make sure that this very pleasant activity is not harmful to marine animals.

There are regulations that limit how close a boat may get to a whale. The speed limit in whale feeding areas is also controlled. Belugas are given special treatment because the beluga population in the St. Lawrence is endangered. Boats are forbidden from approaching them because the Estuary is a beluga calving ground, and there may be mothers with their young around. The Saguenay–St. Lawrence Marine Park was created to protect marine mammals, and boating activity is restricted.

Educating people on boats plays a very important part in protecting these marine mammals. By getting to know whales well and understanding their needs, we can learn to be around them without disturbing them. Whales don't come to the St. Lawrence to entertain us, but to replenish their energy reserves so they can survive the next winter. That is why we must enjoy them from a respectful distance.

Identifying the Whales of the St. Lawrence

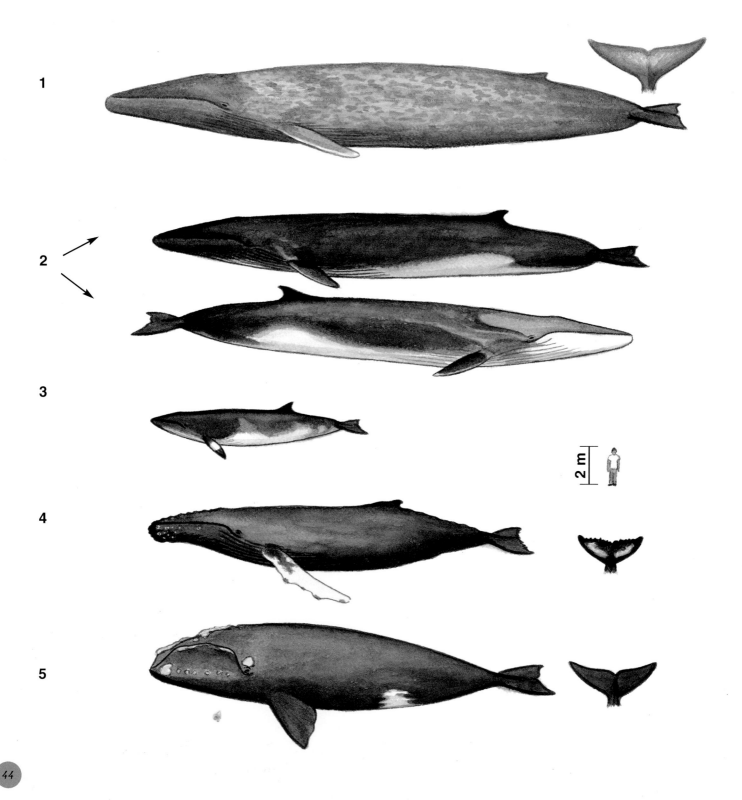

1

2

3

4

5

2 m

very summer, the St. Lawrence River is home to a greater diversity of whale species than any other region. Over ten different migrating species can be found in this feeding area. Each species has its own unique features that allow us to identify it.

Match each whale with the correct definition and check your answers at the bottom of the page. We have drawn a tail beside the species that shows their flukes when they dive.

A. The **fin whale** has asymmetrical coloring on its head.

B. The **sperm whale** has a massive squarish head.

C. The **white-sided dolphin** has a yellow patch on the rear.

D. An adult **beluga** is white and a young beluga is gray.

E. The **right whale** has callosities on its head.

F. The **harbor porpoise** is the smallest cetacean.

G. The **minke whale** has a white patch on its pectoral fin.

H. The **humpback whale**'s dorsal fin is on a hump.

I. The **white-beaked dolphin** has a white muzzle.

J. The **pilot whale** has a hooked dorsal fin.

K. The **blue whale** is the largest cetacean.

L. The **northern bottlenose** whale has a bulbous forehead and a pronounced beak.

M. The male **killer whale** has a long dorsal fin.

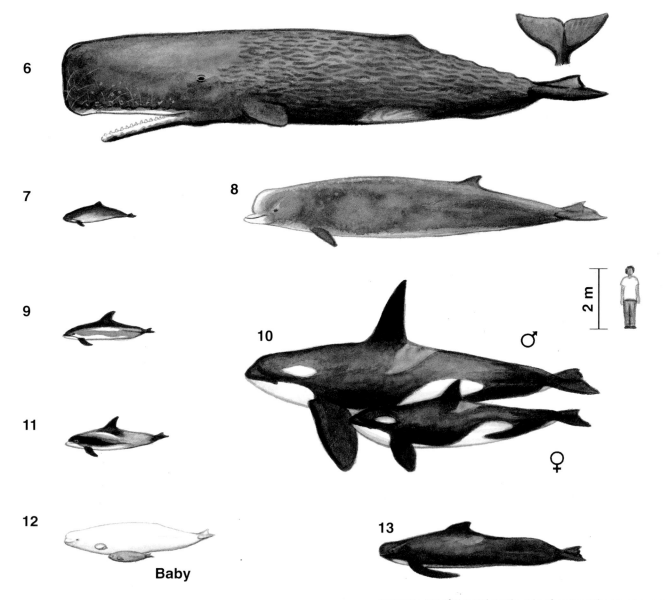

6

7   8

9   10   ♂   2 m

11

12   13

Baby

Answers : A2, B6, C9, D12, E5, F7, G3, H4, I11, J13, K1, L8, M10

45

Resources

Books

Beaulieu, V.I., and P. Couture. *Les gens du fleuve*. Quebec City: Stanké, 1993.

Béland, Pierre. *Le Béluga, l'adieu aux baleines*. Montreal: Libre Expression, 1996.

Breton, Mimi. *Guide to Watching Whales in Canada*. Ottawa: Fisheries and Oceans, 1986.

Cohat, Yves. *Vie et mort des baleines*. Paris: Gallimard. Collection découvertes, 1986.

Cousteau, J.Y., and Y. Paccalet. *La planète des baleines*. Paris: Éditions Robert Laffont, 1986.

Fontaine, P.-H. *Whales of the North Atlantic: Biology and Ecology*. Quebec City: MultiMondes, 1998.

Fontaine, P.-M. *Quelques aspects de l'écologie du marsouin commun (Phocoena phocoena) de l'estuaire et du golfe du Saint-Laurent*. Quebec City: Bibliothèque Scientifique de l'Université de Laval, 1992.

Gremm. "Programme d'interprétation du Groupe de recherche et d'éducation sur le milieu marin, Croisière aux baleines et Croisières sur la rivière Saguenay." 1990.

Hoyt, Erich. *Seasons of the Whale*. Montreal: Broquet, 1993.

Hoyt, Erich. *The Whales of Canada*. Ontario: Camden House, 1990.

Katona, Steven et al. *A Field Guide to the Whales Porpoises and Seals of the Gulf of Maine and Eastern Canada*. 3rd ed. New York: Scribners and Sons, 1983.

Lapointe, Gatien. *Ode au Saint-Laurent*. Trois-Rivières: Les éditions du Zéphyr, 1985.

Michaud, Robert. *Rencontre avec les baleines du Saint-Laurent*. Tadoussac: Gremm, 1993.

Michaud, R., and S. BAKER. "Le béluga du Saint-Laurent, un animal social." Recherche présentée au Biodôme de Montréal dans le cadre d'une exposition sur le béluga du Saint-Laurent," 1996.

Rossignol, Anne. *L'estuaire maritime et le golfe du Saint-Laurent, carnet d'océanographie*. Rimouski: INRS-Oceanology, 1998.

Sears, Richard. *The Blue Whale: A Catalogue of Individuals from the Western North Atlantic (Gulf of St. Lawrence)*. St. Lambert: MICS, 1987.

Sylvestre, Jean-Pierre. *Baleines et Cachalots*. Switzerland: Delachaux et Niestlé, 1989.

Films

Belhumeur, A. *La complainte du béluga*. Montreal: Imagerie PB Ltée, 1989.

Belhumeur, A., and J. Lemire. *Recontreavec les baleines du Sainte-Laurent*. Montreal: Poly-Productions ltée and Les Productions Ciné-Bio, 1996.

Lemire, J., and A. Belhumeur. *Le mystère de la baleine*. Montreal: Imagerie PB Ltée, 1998.

Websites

The Group for Research and Education on Marine Mammals: www.gremm.org

Mingan Island Cetacean Study: www.rorqual.com

Whalenet: http://whale.wheelock.edu

Whales Online: www.whales-online.org

Index